Spotlight on the
MAYA, AZTEC, and INCA CIVILIZATIONS

Ancient INCA CULTURE

Kristen Rajczak Nelson

PowerKiDS press™

NEW YORK

Published in 2017 by The Rosen Publishing Group, Inc.
29 East 21st Street, New York, NY 10010

Editor: Sarah Machajewski

Photo Credits: Cover DEA /A. DAGLI ORTI/De Agostini/Getty Images; pp. 4, 6 https://commons.wikimedia.org/
wiki/File:Inca_Empire.svg; p. 5 Danita Delimont/Gallo Images/Getty Images; p. 7 ATicuS/Moment/
Getty Images; p. 9 BERTRAND LANGLOIS/AFP/Getty Images; p. 10 Rafal Cichawa/Shutterstock.com;
p. 11 AIZAR RALDES/AFP/Getty Images; p. 12 Geraint Rowland Photography/Moment/Getty Images;
p. 13 Cultura RM Exclusive/Philip Lee Harvey/Cultura Exclusive/Getty Images; p. 15 hadynyah/Vetta/Getty Images;
p. 16 https://commons.wikimedia.org/wiki/File:Tupa-inca-tunic.png; p. 17 hadynyah/E+/Getty Images;
p. 18 https://commons.wikimedia.org/wiki/File:Cusco_Coricancha_Inti-Huasi_main_view.jpg;
p. 19 https://commons.wikimedia.org/wiki/File:Willkawaman_cathedral.jpg; pp. 20, 28 Hulton Archive/
Getty Images; p. 21 Alex Bramwell/Moment/Getty Images; p. 22 https://en.wikipedia.org/wiki/File:Mur_Inca_
Décembre_2007.jpg; p. 23 https://en.wikipedia.org/wiki/File:Walls_at_Sacsayhuaman.jpg; p. 24 Pola Damonte/
Shutterstock.com; p. 25 Christian Wilkinson/Shutterstock.com; p. 27 Werner Forman/Universal Images Group/
Getty Images; p. 29 https://en.wikipedia.org/wiki/File:Funeralesdeatahualpa_luismontero.png.

Library of Congress Cataloging-in-Publication Data

Names: Nelson, Kristen Rajczak, author.
Title: Ancient Inca culture / Kristen Rajczak Nelson.
Description: New York : PowerKids Press, 2016. | Series: Spotlight on the
  Maya, Aztec, and Inca civilizations | Includes index.
Identifiers: LCCN 2016000861 | ISBN 9781499419283 (pbk.) | ISBN 9781499419313 (library bound) | ISBN
9781499419290 (6 pack)
Subjects: LCSH: Incas--Juvenile literature.
Classification: LCC F3429 .N428 2016 | DDC 985/.01--dc23
LC record available at http://lccn.loc.gov/2016000861

CPSIA Compliance Information: Batch #BS16PK: For further information contact Rosen Publishing, New York, New York at 1-800-237-9932.

CONTENTS

WHO ARE THE INCA?

For almost 100 years, the Inca Empire was one of the most powerful, impressive civilizations in the world. It reached its greatest size during the early 1500s, stretching about 2,500 miles (4,023 km) along the Pacific coast of South America. About 12 million people lived within the boundaries of the Inca Empire. Many were conquered peoples who had also been living in the Andes Mountains.

Though short-lived, the Inca Empire developed a rich culture that helped the government and military become very powerful. An extensive road system and inventive agricultural techniques allowed the empire to supply and support its large population. Well-crafted architecture and functional art were more than just tools for living—they made daily life in the Inca Empire beautiful.

SOUTH AMERICA

INCA EMPIRE

Much of what is known about the ancient Inca comes from archaeology, or the study of past cultures through their remains. Archaeologists have spent many years uncovering Inca ruins and **artifacts**.

Learning about Inca culture hasn't been easy, as the Spanish destroyed many parts of the empire when they arrived in the 16th century. However, the details known today tell the story of a culture that honored its gods, made beautiful items, and developed remarkable skills.

FOUNDING AN EMPIRE

Around the year AD 1100, a **drought** in the Andes helped bring down a group of strong lords who had ruled the region. Leaders of tribes in the area began fighting over water and food, which caused many people to flee high into the mountains. One group of farmers stayed in their valley instead. They were the Inca, and they lived in small villages and stood together against enemies.

Tradition says the Inca originally lived in the village of Paqari-tampu, which is about 15 miles (24 km) south of Cuzco. A leader named Manco Capac led the Inca people to Cuzco, which became the capital of their settlement. The Inca had plenty of resources, which allowed them to look beyond the valley to other settlements nearby—and take them over.

CUZCO

SOUTH AMERICA

The city of Cuzco is one of the oldest **inhabited** cities in the Western Hemisphere. It survives today in southern Peru.

The Inca really began expanding during the 14th century. The civilization truly became an empire around 1438, when the ninth emperor, Pachacuti, began conquering peoples south of Cuzco.

INSIDE INCA SOCIETY

Inca society was divided into classes. The Inca emperor was called the Sapa Inca, and he was the most powerful person in the Inca Empire. Below him was the royal class. It was made of the emperor's sons and family. Next was the noble class, which included more royal family members, priests, and leaders in the empire. The lowest social class was everyone else—farmers, craftspeople, and servants.

When the Sapa Inca died, his son became emperor and inherited all the powers that came with it. Beginning under Pachacuti, the new emperor had to gain his own wealth, mostly by conquering new lands. Pachacuti set this in motion as part of a greater focus on worshipping ancestors.

Pachacuti made other decisions that shaped much of Inca culture. For example, he made it so that Inca rulers continued to own their land and money after they died. Their descendants continued living off what the ruler owned during his life.

The Inca mummified and worshipped their dead rulers, which showed they were still an important part of the government. However, the Spanish destroyed the mummies of Sapa Incas, so the mummy pictured here was not likely a ruler.

Though there was a wealthy upper class, the largest part of the Inca population worked as laborers and farmers. The culture valued hard work and became strong partly because everything was shared among its citizens. For example, Inca farmers grew more food than they needed. They were allowed to keep a part of their harvest. One part was given to priests to use in ceremonies. One part was given to the Sapa Inca. The government then kept the food in storehouses called *qollqa*. The extra food was used during times of **famine**, which meant no one in Inca society went hungry.

The Inca Empire's farmers were an important part of making the civilization great because the Inca economy was based on its bountiful harvests of corn, potatoes, squash, peanuts, **cassava**, cotton, and more. Historians have found the Inca culture to be very organized, especially in keeping track of growing and storing crops.

QOLLQA

In traditional villages found in the Andes, neighbors helped each other in their fields. This idea, called *ayni* in the Quechua language, was adopted in Inca culture to the great benefit of the empire.

THE CULTURE OF DAILY LIFE

The Inca's agricultural success was proof of the society's resourcefulness. Farmers in the Inca Empire grew their crops on **terraces** cut into the Andes Mountains. The terraces were surrounded by stone walls and filled with dirt. This practice allowed the Inca to farm on the steep mountain slopes found in their empire.

In addition, the Inca raised animals and used them in many parts of life. The Inca captured llamas and alpaca herds owned by other lords living in the Andes because they were so important. Both animals were eaten and their hides were used to make clothing. Llamas could also carry

Inca laborers built irrigation canals, or manmade waterways used to keep crops watered, on the slopes of the Andes to carry water down from the peaks.

up to 70 pounds (32 kg) at a time, making them great pack animals, and especially valuable to the military.

Caring for the fields and animals was hard work, but in exchange, everyone was provided for. This was done on purpose. The Inca rulers wanted their people to be too busy and too well fed to **rebel**.

Everyone had to get married in the Inca culture, mostly because the Inca government only gave land to married couples. Because of this, couples also married for life. Both men and women worked hard to ensure their family—and the empire—was provided for.

At home, men commonly worked in the fields or at a certain trade. They also had to take part in *mit'a* service, which took them away from home to work for the empire. They moved goods throughout the empire, built buildings and bridges, or served in the military. Some men also mined the gold, silver, and copper the Inca Empire became known for.

Women also had to perform a service, but it was done at home. They **wove** cloth for the empire. Women also cooked, cleaned, worked in the fields, and took care of their children.

Inca women often carried their babies while they worked. Here, a Peruvian woman weaves with her child on her back, much like her ancestors would have done.

ANCIENT WEAVERS

Weaving was an important part of life in the Andes long before the Inca Empire rose to power. The Inca perfected the kind of weaving they found most useful and are historically known for producing some of the most beautiful **textiles** ever made. They used cotton and wool from alpacas and llamas to make cloth. The quality of the cloth used for someone's clothing showed their social class.

INCA TEXTILE

A group of the most beautiful women in the empire, called the Chosen Women, were taught to be the best weavers. They used wool from animals called vicuñas and guanacos to make clothing for the Sapa Inca and the nobles. The cloth was dyed bright colors and had details made with gold and silver thread. Fine cloth was one of the most treasured items among the Inca, and it helped expand the empire. Fine cloth was commonly offered to the leader of a group the Inca wanted to rule. If it was accepted, the group pledged loyalty to the Inca emperor.

STATE RELIGION

Much of the art made by the Inca had a **religious** meaning. This shows just how important spiritual beliefs were to the Inca. For example, the textiles they made honored an earth goddess. The Inca believed in **animism** and some magic. Many of their ceremonies worshipped nature.

The Inca Empire had a state religion that honored the sun god, Inti. He was said to help crops grow, so farmers

SUN TEMPLE IN CUZCO

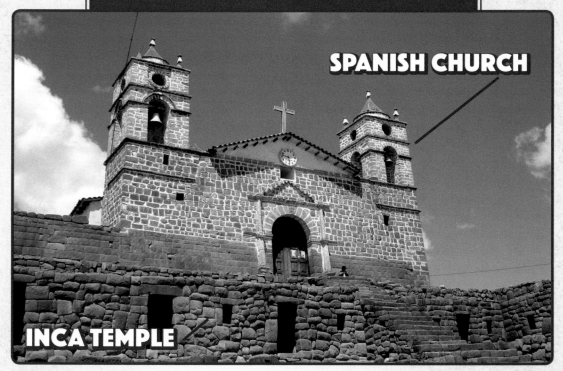

Temples such as this one at Vilcashuamán were an important part of the Inca state religion. Spanish conquerors often built on top of the remains of former Inca temples.

SPANISH CHURCH

INCA TEMPLE

paid him special attention. One of the most well-known Inca temples is the Sun Temple in Cuzco. It was built to honor Inti. The Inca built temples to other gods, too. Priests lived at the temples, prepared to heal people, hear confessions, and more.

Not everyone in the Inca Empire held the beliefs of the state religion alone. The Inca conquered many people, so other native religions were allowed as long as the people also took care of their Inca religious duties.

Each day, the Inca made **sacrifices** of corn to the sun god. On important days, they might sacrifice llamas, guinea pigs, or other animals they used as food. People were sacrificed to the gods at times, too, such as when the empire faced military defeat or if food was scarce. Sometimes, these sacrifices were children.

The Inca state religion also included festivals, though. They followed a religious calendar with months that were 30 days long. Each month had a festival. These festivals were likely designed by the empire to keep workers happy.

In this painting, the Inca people celebrate the Great Feast of the Sun.

People were also sacrificed when a new emperor came into power. They may have been killed on an altar like this one.

The main population of the Inca Empire worked hard in the fields every day, and festivals offered a few days of fun. They included dancing, music, lots of food, a beer-like drink called *chicha*, and religious celebrations. Festivals also offered leaders the chance to communicate the greatness of the empire to all their workers, making them proud of military success and their emperor.

INCA ARCHITECTURE

A great **fortress** sits high atop a mountain in the Andes. It has remained standing despite hundreds of years of wind and other weather. It's called Machu Picchu, and its survival shows just how skilled Inca builders were.

The Inca built mostly with stone. The stones were shaped to fit together like puzzle pieces. In order to shape stones and put them into place for the huge temples, fortresses, and other buildings, many workers were needed. One account says 20 men worked for a whole year on shaping one stone for its place in a building.

Homes in the Inca culture were commonly made of stone or adobe, which are bricks made of dried earth.

Perhaps more impressive than the tight-fitting **joins** of Inca architecture were how the buildings were decorated. The Inca covered some buildings, especially temples, with gold and silver. The Sun Temple, or Coricancha, had a garden made entirely of silver and gold, from the dirt and plants to the llamas and shepherds standing in it.

One of the greatest feats of building the Inca accomplished was a system of roads. Two main roads ran north to south for thousands of miles. Smaller roads ran between them. Along their length were small temples, storehouses, and places for travelers to rest. The Inca built tunnels and bridges across rivers and **ravines**.

Use of the roads was limited to the government and the military. It was the fastest way to travel throughout the large empire. The roads were also the fastest way to communicate. A group of runners passed messages along, in a system similar to a relay race, until the messages reached the places they needed to go.

The roads leading to Machu Picchu feature switchbacks, or sharp curves. Roads with switchbacks are easier to travel than steep paths that go directly up the side of a mountain.

All the work to build roads and structures high in the Andes was done without modern tools. The Inca didn't have the wheel or metal tools, making their success even more impressive.

LIVING LANGUAGE

People living in the Inca Empire spoke a group of related languages collectively called Quechua. Forms of Quechua had existed in Andean communities, including much of modern Peru, for hundreds of years before the Inca Empire was founded. The Inca then spread it into new areas, such as present-day Bolivia, as the empire grew. However, not all Quechua speakers could understand each other. The language changed and developed in different parts of the empire. So, while many Inca from different areas could understand one another, others that lived farther apart likely could not.

For as developed as the Inca culture was, the people didn't use a written language. They did use a system of colorful, knotted strings called quipu to show numbers and keep track of taxes, food, and labor. Some people think the quipu might have been used to send messages as well, but that has yet to be proven.

The length and color of string and the type of knots used to create a quipu all meant something to the person who received it, such as how many llamas were accounted for or the amount of crops in a storehouse.

CONQUERED

During the late 1520s, a small group of Inca met Spanish explorers for the first time. The Inca had gold and silver aboard their raft and told the Spanish their civilization had much more. The Spanish, including explorer Francisco Pizarro, accompanied the Inca south to learn more.

The Spanish were drawn to the Inca Empire by its wealth. The Spanish even dug up graves to steal gold and silver from the Inca.

Atahualpa, the last Sapa Inca before the Spanish conquest, is pictured here during his funeral. He was captured and killed by Pizarro.

At the same time, a terrible civil war broke out in the Inca Empire over who would be emperor. Pizarro took advantage of the empire's weakness. With permission from the queen of Spain, Pizarro conquered the Inca with an army of about 160 men. They used guns, something the Inca didn't have.

The Spanish brought another powerful weapon with them: disease. The already battle-torn empire became weaker as many Andean people died from European illnesses their bodies couldn't fight.

While the Inca fled from and fought with the Spanish, their amazing road system and beautiful buildings weren't cared for. Temples were destroyed by the Spanish, taken apart for the gold and silver decorating them.

BEYOND THE EMPIRE

After the Spanish conquest in 1533, Spanish culture began to mix with that of the Inca Empire. The languages began to borrow words from one another. Spanish priests forced the native inhabitants to practice Christianity instead of their traditional religions.

Today, the influence of both the Spanish culture and the Inca Empire remain in the descendants of the ancient Inca. Many still live in the high mountains of the Andes, speaking similar languages and trying to make a living by weaving and farming in the traditional ways of the ancient Inca culture. However, many don't make enough money to feed their families.

The culture of the ancient Inca survives in their descendants, but also in the ruins that remain throughout South America. Archaeologists and historians continue to study the remains of Inca buildings to find out more about the fascinating, vibrant culture of the Inca.

GLOSSARY

animism (AA-nuh-mih-suhm): The belief that everything, both living and nonliving, has a spirit.

artifact (AHR-tuh-fahkt): A simple tool or ornament made by people in the past.

cassava (kuh-SAH-vuh): A root vegetable.

drought (DROWT): A long period of little or no rain.

famine (FAA-muhn): An extreme lack of food.

fortress (FOHR-truhs): A large, strong building or structure around a town.

inhabit (ihn-HAA-biht): To live in a place.

join (JOYN): The place where two things meet.

ravine (ruh-VEEN): A deep, narrow gorge with steep sides.

rebel (rih-BEHL): To oppose a government.

religious (rih-LIH-juhs): Having to do with religion, or the belief in gods or traditions one follows.

sacrifice (SAA-kruh-fyce): Someone or something that is offered to a god or ruler. Also, the offering of someone or something in this fashion.

terrace (TAIR-uhs): A flat area built into a slope, often to provide farmland.

textile (TEHK-styl): Cloth, or a fiber used to make cloth.

weave (WEEV): To make cloth by crossing strands of thread or yarn over and over.

INDEX

PRIMARY SOURCE LIST

Page 5: Ruins of the Saksaywaman citadel. Built by the Killke culture around 1100 and expanded by the Inca around 1200. Stone. Located near Cuzco, Peru.

Page 10: Inca ruins at Pinkuylluna. Built by the Inca. ca. 15th century. Stone. Located near Ollantaytambo, Peru.

Page 16: All T'oqapu tunic from the Inca civilization. Creator unknown. Wool and cotton. Created between 1450 and 1540. Now kept at the Dumbarton Oaks Library, Washington, D.C.

Page 22: Inca wall. Built by the Inca. Stone. Date unknown. Located in Cuzco, Peru.

WEBSITES

Due to the changing nature of Internet links, PowerKids Press has developed an online list of websites related to the subject of this book. This site is updated regularly. Please use this link to access the list: www.powerkidslinks.com/soac/incc